Funny Fishes

Funny Fishes

Sara Swan Miller

Watts LIBRARY

Franklin Watts
A Division of Grolier Publishing
New York • London • Hong Kong • Sydney
Danbury, Connecticut

Note to readers: Definitions for words in **bold** can be found in the Glossary at the back of this book.

Photographs ©: Aaron Norman: cover, 9 bottom; Animals Animals/Zig Leszczynski: 14; Corbis-Bettmann: 22 (Brandon D. Cole), 5 top, 17 (Jeffrey L. Rotman); Dembinsky Photo Assoc./Gary Meszaros: 8; Franklin J. Viola: 9 top, 20, 29; National Geographic Image Collection/George Grall: 13; Norbert Wu Photography: 23; Photo Researchers: 45 (A.W. Ambler), 46 (Stephen Dalton), 32 (Nigel J. Dennis), 38 (Aaron Ferster), 40 (Fletcher & Baylis), 24, 25 (Tom & Pat Leeson), 34 (Tom McHugh), 36, 37 (Tom McHugh/Steinhart Aquarium), 10, 11 (William H. Mullins), 44 (Mark Smith), 5 bottom, 15 (Dr. Paul A. Zahl); Stone/Daniel J. Cox: 2; Visuals Unlimited: 35, 18, 27 (Patrice Ceisel), 30 (John D. Cunningham), 6 (Jeff Greenberg), 48, 49 (Ken Lucas), 19 (Glenn M. Oliver), 21 (Fred Rhode), 41 (Brian Rogers), 12 (Rob & Ann Simpson).

The photograph on the cover shows a mudskipper. The photograph opposite the title page shows several chum salmon trying to jump over a waterfall in Alaska.

Visit Franklin Watts on the Internet at:
http://publishing.grolier.com

Library of Congress Cataloging-in-Publication Data

Miller, Sara Swan
    Funny Fishes / by Sara Swan Miller
       p.   cm.— (Watts Library)
    Includes bibliographical references and index.
    Summary: Portrays several species of fishes that have unusual appearances, habitats, or behaviors
    ISBN 0-531-11797-9 (lib. bdg.)   0-531-13982-4 (pbk.)
    1. Fishes—Juvenile literature. [1. Fishes.] I. Title. II. Series.
QL605.3. M56 2000
597—dc21   99-057308

GROLIER
PUBLISHING 1 2 3 4 5 6 7 8 9 10 R 10 09 08 07 06 05 04 03 02 01

Contents

Most people can recognize a fish.

Chapter One

What Is a Fish?

Do you know what a fish is? You might just say "an animal that lives in the water." That's true of course, but it doesn't tell us enough information. Not every animal that lives in the water is a fish. Frogs are not fish. Neither are lobsters, crabs, oysters, octopuses, squid, or sea jellies. So what makes those animals different from fish? Scientists organize plants and animals into categories according to their differences and their similarities. If you've learned about fishes

"Fish" or "Fishes"

What's the right word to use when you're talking about more than one fish? If you're talking about several fish of the same kind, the plural is "fish." If you're talking about several different kinds of fish, the plural is "fishes."

in school, you may know some of the qualities that make them different from animals in the other groups. So suppose your teacher asked you, "What is a fish?" What would you say?

You would probably start by saying that a fish is an animal that lives in bodies of water such as streams, lakes, or oceans. Fishes are **vertebrates**, which means that they belong to the group of animals that has backbones. Having a backbone and an internal skeleton make a fish different from many other water creatures.

A fish swims with the help of fins. It has two **pectoral fins** on its sides, and two **pelvic fins** on its belly. On its back and near its tail are two more fins—they act like the keel on a boat and keep it steady. The one on its back is the **dorsal fin**, and the one underneath is the **anal fin**. Fishes can glide through the water because they are streamlined. Most have a tapering nose pointing forward and a torpedo-shaped body stretching out behind. Its finned tail drives a fish forward. The body of a fish is covered with small, transparent plates called **scales**.

It's easy to see the fins on this brook trout.

Since fishes spend their lives underwater, they can't breathe air with lungs the way people do. Instead, most fishes have **gills** on the sides of their heads that filter oxygen out of the water. Female fishes lays eggs, which are fertilized in the water by the male's **milt**. Some fishes make a nest and guard their eggs, but most of them just lay their eggs and swim away.

Scientists organize fishes into three different groups. The most primitive group is the jawless fishes. Fishes in the second group, which includes sharks and rays, have skeletons made of cartilage instead of bone. The third group is made up of the bony fishes, which include bass and perch.

If you came up with all those fishy facts, you know all the "rules" that help you distinguish a fish from other animals—but some fishes don't follow all those rules. Did you ever see a fish that walks about on land? Can you imagine a fish that doesn't lay eggs? Can a sea horse really be a fish?

Strange as it may seem, all these peculiar creatures really are fishes—and there are many other funny fishes. The world of fishes can be full of surprises!

The Size of Things

The largest fish is the whale shark (top). It can grow up to 50 feet (15 meters) long—as long as a freight locomotive. The smallest fish in the world is the Filipino dwarf pygmy goby (bottom). It's about as big as your fingertip.

9

This smallmouth bass has a "normal" fish shape.

Chapter Two

That Doesn't Look Like a Fish!

What does a fish look like? When you think of a fish, you probably picture it as "fish-shaped," like a trout or a bass. You expect a slim, sleek, streamlined body for efficient swimming. You probably expect it to have scales, a tail, and the right number of fins on its body. Many of the bony fishes look exactly the way we expect—but others hardly look like fish at all.

Sea Horses

A sea horse looks nothing like a regular fish. Its scientific name, *Hippocampus*, means "bent horse," but parts of it resemble other animals too. Its head is shaped like a tiny horse's head, but it also has a snout, like an anteater. It has a long, flexible tail like a monkey, and large swiveling eyes like a chameleon.

A sea horse doesn't swim like other fish, either. It swims upright, waving the dorsal fin on its back. Small pectoral fins help it steer, but it has no other fins at all. Instead of a tail fin, the sea horse has a long, grasping tail. It winds its tail around seaweed and stays motionless, waiting for tiny animals, fish larvae, or eggs to come its way. Then it sucks them up with its narrow, tubelike mouth.

A lined sea horse hides in the coral.

Keeping upright helps to protect the sea horse. It looks just like the sea grasses and coral branches it hides in, so it blends in well with its surroundings. A sea horse can also change its colors to match whatever it's hiding in, from gray or black to bright orange or yellow. As long as it stays perfectly still, most of its enemies don't even know it's there.

A sea horse is strange in other ways too. It doesn't have overlapping scales like most fishes. Instead, its scales have **evolved**, or changed slowly over many generations, into bony rings. These

12

rings help protect the sea horse, as do its unusual eyes. Like a chameleon, a sea horse can turn its eyes independently, so that it can look in two directions at once. It can search for food and watch for danger at the same time.

Perhaps the strangest thing about the sea horse is that the male gives birth to the young. First, the female lays several hundred eggs in a pouch on his belly. He **fertilizes** the eggs with his sperm, and the sea horse **embryos** develop inside his pouch. The embryos live off the food stored in their individual yolk sacs. In a few weeks, the young sea horses are ready to be born, although they are no more than $^1/_2$ inch (1 centimeter) long. When that time comes, the father grabs onto a seaweed stem and begins bending backward and forward. Soon, the tiny sea horses start shooting out of his pouch.

A male sea horse giving birth.

All Kinds of Sea Horses

About 35 species of sea horses are found in oceans around the world, ranging in size from 1.5 inches (3 cm) to 12 inches (30 cm) long.

The Pipefish

A pipefish is another fish that you might think looks peculiar—if you can find it at all! The pipefish live along the coasts of eastern North America. This long, slender fish rests upright among eelgrasses and other tall seaweeds. With its green and brown coloring and grasslike shape, it can easily hide in the seaweed.

A northern pipefish hides among some seaweed.

The pipefish is related to the sea horse. Picture a pipefish curved into a sea horse shape and you will see how similar they are. Like the sea horse, the pipefish has a long, tubular snout with a small mouth at the end. It uses its snout to slurp up small **prey**, including tiny shrimp. Like the sea horse, the pipefish has only a dorsal fin, two small pectoral fins, and a tiny anal fin. Also like the sea horse, the pipefish has no scales. Although it looks soft and helpless at first glance, the pipefish is covered with bony plates. This covering makes it hard for a pipefish to bend, but it is a good defense.

A pipefish is like a sea horse in another way too. The male usually hatches the eggs and gives birth to

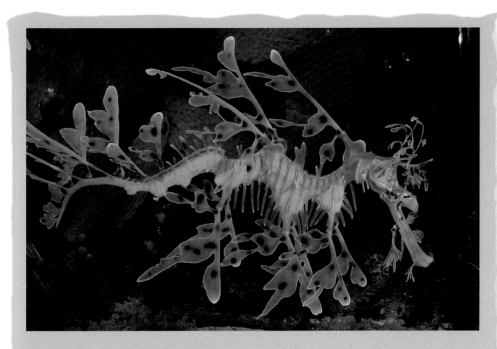

A Really Weird Pipefish

The leafy seadragon of Australia is covered with fleshy flaps and long feelers that blend in with seaweed, and help it hide from predators.

the young. At mating time, the male and female court by swimming upright past each other several times. The male then begins rubbing the female's abdomen with his snout. Finally, they twist around each other, and the female lays her eggs in the male's pouch. The males of some pipefish species don't have a pouch, so the female just sticks the eggs to his belly.

The male carries the eggs until they hatch. Then, if the eggs are stuck to the father's belly, the young can just swim away. If they're in the father's pouch, the pouch bursts open, and the young swim free.

The Box Fish

A box fish doesn't look much like a fish. It looks more like a box with fins. It doesn't have scales like other fishes, either. Instead, it is covered by a bony, hard shell, called a **carapace**. The carapace protects the box fish from its enemies, but the shell makes it hard for the box fish to bend or wiggle.

Box fish swim slowly along on the sandy floors of tropical seas, feeding on **algae**, shrimp, and sponges. For some box fishes, like the speckled box fish, armor isn't the only defense. If it is attacked, the speckled box fish releases a cloud of poison and swims away, leaving its attacker to die. Some people keep speckled box fish in home aquariums, but that can cause a real problem. If a box fish is frightened, it will release its poison. Since it can't swim away, it kills everything in the aquarium—including itself!

Another odd thing about box fish is that they can change their sex. If there are too many females and not enough males, some of the drab-looking females turn themselves into bright-colored males. This unusual ability ensures that there will be just the right number of each sex to mate, lay eggs, and carry on the species.

Armor from the Ocean?

The carapace of the box fish is such good protection that some people used to use box fish shells to make armor.

Puffer fish

The puffer fish, a relative of the box fish, has an unusual way of scaring off its enemies. It blows itself up and sticks out hundreds of spines to scare away enemies. The puffer fish is also highly poisonous—but some people eat them as a delicacy!

Garden Eels

Imagine that you are diving in the Caribbean Sea and you come across a beautiful garden of grasses swaying in the water current. You swim closer. Suddenly, the "garden" shrinks and disappears—those "grasses" were actually a colony of garden eels!

Garden eels don't look or act like most other fishes. Each garden eel uses a hard, fleshy point near its tail to dig a tunnel in the sandy ocean floor. Then it anchors its long, thin body in its tunnel. Several garden eels in a cluster look a lot like sea grasses. It's a good trick—bigger fish don't realize that the clump of "grasses" would be a tasty meal.

A garden of garden eels waiting for prey to pass by.

Electric Eels

The electric eel of South America can deliver a jolt of electricity strong enough to stun a human being, kill a small fish, or light a neon bulb.

If an enemy gets too close, the garden eels sink down into the safety of their tunnels. When the coast is clear, the garden eels rise back out and sway in the currents again. When unsuspecting small animals come floating or swimming by, the garden eels gobble them up.

Many eels have no scales on their bodies, while others have scales so tiny that you need a microscope to see them. Garden eels have no pelvic fins, and their other fins are small, but they don't really need fins. They stay anchored in their holes, waiting for little morsels to float by.

Toad Fishes

If you saw a toad fish lurking on the ocean floor off Central America, you would probably think that it was a toad! It's a small, sluggish fish with a thick body and a wide head. Like a toad, it has eyes on the top of its head, and a wide mouth.

A toad fish is hard to spot on the ocean floor. Its squat body and dull colors help it blend in with the sand and rocks. Don't let its fat, slow looks fool you, though. The toad fish is a fierce **predator**. When unsuspecting prey swims by, the toad fish can snatch it instantly and devour it with its little sharp teeth.

One species of toad fish from around South America is extremely poisonous. Sacs under its skin feed venom into hollow spines on its dorsal fin and gill covers. If you stepped on one of these toad fish, the spines would act like hypodermic

The toad fish is well named.

Deadly Stone Fish

The stone fish looks like a harmless rock, but its venom can kill a human being. It has the strongest venom in the fish world.

needles, injecting venom into your foot. The poison might not kill you, but it would make you very ill.

A Look at Hagfish

It's hard to believe a hagfish is a fish. It looks more like a large, slimy worm. A hagfish is one of the jawless fishes. It has no scales, no paired fins, and, as the name implies, no jaws. It has no eyes, either, just two depressions where you would expect its eyes to be. Other areas on its head and tail can sense light and dark.

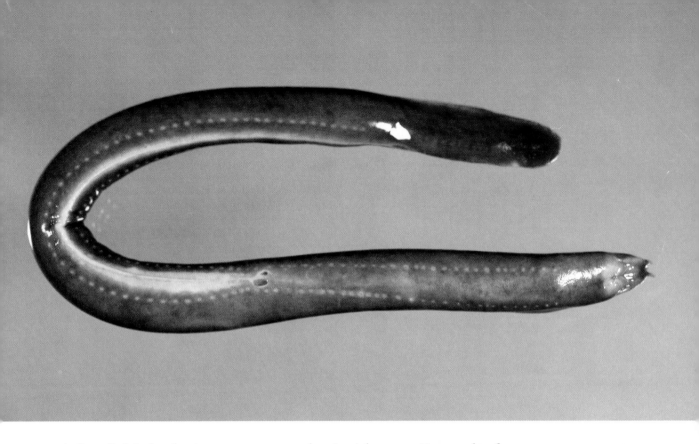

A hagfish's body is strange on the inside too. Instead of bones, it has soft, flexible cartilage, like the cartilage that forms the outer part of your ears. The hagfish has no stomach at all, but has six hearts! One heart pushes blood through the tiny blood vessels in its gills to extract oxygen from the water. Two hearts help speed the blood after it has passed through the gills. Another heart pumps blood into its liver. Finally, it has two small hearts near its tail.

Why does the hagfish need so many hearts? Unlike other fishes, a hagfish's blood isn't always inside its blood vessels. Some of it collects in open spaces called **sinuses**. The hagfish needs a heart behind each sinus to pump blood on to the rest of its body.

The strange hagfish looks like a big worm.

21

Although it has no eyes, no jaws, and no stomach, a hagfish is a successful **parasite**. It attaches itself to larger fish and feeds from them. A nostril above its mouth helps it smell. When the hagfish smells a dead or dying fish, it swims swiftly toward it and fixes its round, tentacled mouth on the fish's side. Then it quickly drills a hole inside the fish with its rasping tongue and eats its way inside its victim.

Thirty-two species of hagfishes live in the cold oceans of the world. The North American hagfish has an unusual way of defending itself from predators. It produces a huge amount of slime that predators don't like. A North American hagfish produces enough slime to fill a bucket in one minute.

Another strange thing about a hagfish is that it can tie itself up. When it's trying to chew its way into a very large

Someone has been handling a mucus-covered hagfish.

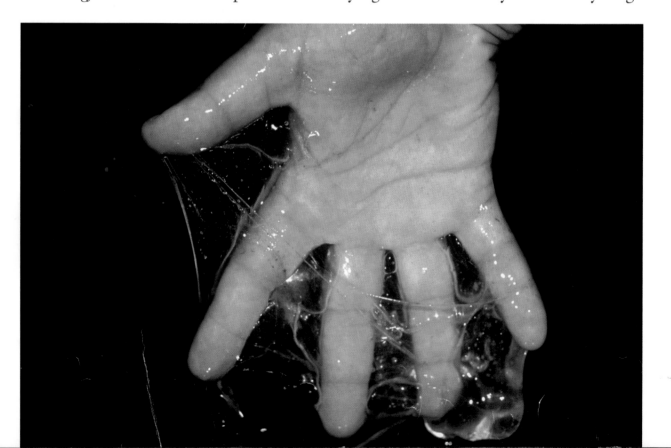

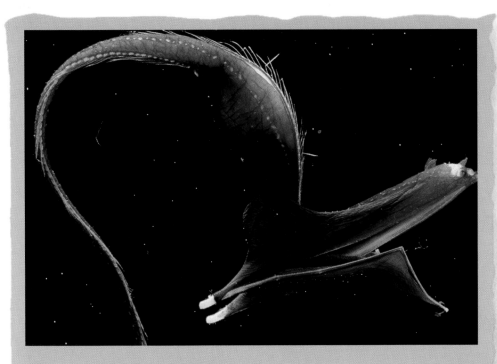

Strange Deepwater Fish

Many strange-looking fish live in the deep ocean. The anglerfish has a body part that it dangles over its mouth to lure fish inside. It looks like a fishing rod baited with a wriggling worm. Most deepwater fish have very large mouths with long, sharp teeth. The gulper eel, which lives in the deep ocean, has a really huge mouth and a tiny, thin body. It seems to be *all* mouth!

fish, it ties itself into a knot. This gives it the leverage it needs to push itself inside. Knotting its body up can help it escape predators too, because a knotted-up hagfish may look too big to eat. When too much slime begins to clog its gills, the hagfish wipes it off by sliding its body through the knot. It can't clean the thick slime out of its nostril that way, though, so it sneezes.

*Chinook salmon
heading upstream
to spawn*

Chapter Three

Radical Reproduction

If you've ever seen salmon spawning in a river, you probably have an idea of how fish are "supposed" to breed. Like most fishes, female salmon lay their eggs in the water, and the males fertilize them by releasing milt over them. Then the parents swim away, leaving the eggs and young to develop on their own. Some fishes make nests on the bottom and guard their eggs and young until they're ready to take care of themselves. There are some fishes that have other ways of producing young. Different species have developed ways of reproducing that work in their specific habitats. Some species even give birth like mammals!

Banded Yellow Mouthbrooders

Banded yellow mouthbrooders do lay their eggs in the water, but after the male has fertilized them, the female does a very odd thing. She scoops the eggs into her mouth and holds them there until they hatch several weeks later. All that time, she doesn't eat. Even after the eggs hatch, the young stay in the safety of their mother's mouth for a while.

By the time the young are finally ready to venture forth into their watery world, their mother is very hungry. She hasn't eaten in a long time. The young stay close to their mother, though, and when danger threatens, they zip back into her mouth. When the danger has passed, the mother blows them out of her mouth.

Banded yellow mouthbrooders live in the rivers and lakes of eastern Africa. They are part of a large family of fish called cichlids (SICK-lids). Cichlids live in freshwater in warm places

Those Crazy Cichlids

All cichlid parents take care of their young, though not all of them keep their young in their mouths. Some cichlids just guard the eggs and young, and fan them to keep the water oxygenated. Some lay their eggs in caves and care for the young when they hatch. Others lay their eggs inside snail shells, and then block the opening so predators can't get inside.

all around the globe. Banded yellow mouthbrooders do a good job of protecting their young, but they have one dangerous enemy—another species of cichlid. That cichlid's main source of food is the eggs and young of the mouthbrooders. These predators attack the female mouthbrooder until she is forced to cough up her precious cargo, which they promptly gobble up.

Arawanas

The arawanas of South America also protect their eggs and young inside their mouths. Among arawanas, however, it's the male who does the job. After the female lays her eggs and the

An arawana watches for prey overhead.

Most insects, fish, amphibians, reptiles, and all birds lay eggs that hatch outside of the mother's body. The eggs of some animals hatch inside the mother's body and are born live. The young of other animals, including most mammals, aren't protected by an egg. Instead, they are nurtured inside their mother. They live off nutrients from her body until they are born.

male fertilizes them, he scoops the fertilized eggs gently into a special pouch in his mouth. He can't eat until the young are finally grown and ready to leave several weeks later.

The arawana is unusual in other ways too. It has a very large, scooplike mouth that is directed upward. As it cruises along just under the water's surface, the arawana gulps down anything swimming above, but it doesn't seem to notice prey beneath it.

Arawanas are acrobats. The local people call them "water monkeys," because they leap far out of the water to catch insects, birds, and even bats.

Hammerhead Sharks

Most fishes lay eggs that are fertilized in the water. Some sharks, however, have a completely different way of doing things. The female hammerhead nourishes her embryos inside her body and gives birth to live young like a mammal.

At first, the embryos live off nutrients from a yolk sac. Soon, the empty yolk sac attaches itself to the wall of the shark's uterus and forms a kind of **placenta**, much like that of

a mammal. The yolk sac-placenta brings nutrients from the mother's bloodstream to the embryo and carries off wastes.

It takes nearly a year for the young to develop. When they swim out of their mother's body, the young sharks are already swift and hungry hunters like their parents. If you could get a look at a newborn hammerhead's belly, you would see a small scar where it was attached to its mother by an umbilical cord, like a mammal's bellybutton.

A hammerhead shark uses all its senses to hunt for food.

Strange Egg Cases

Did you ever find a dried-up "mermaid's purse" washed up on the beach? If so, you found an egg case that may have come from a dogfish, a type of shark. The male dogfish fertilizes the female's eggs inside her body, where they grow for a while. Then she lays them in pairs in hard egg cases. Curly tendrils at each corner of the egg case help it cling to seaweed.

A hammerhead has other unusual features, too. Its head is shaped like a huge hammer with one eye and one nostril way out each end of its wide head. This strange arrangement helps it see and smell its fast-moving prey more easily. Other organs help the shark sense electrical fields.

Its acute senses make a hammerhead an excellent hunter. It chases after bony fishes and other sharks, and it loves to eat stingrays! It can find a stingray buried in the sand by sweeping its head back and forth over the ocean bottom like a living metal detector. When the sense organs along the front of its head pick up the smell and electrical fields of its prey, it quickly zeroes in for the kill.

Hammerheads live in oceans all over the world—wherever they can find stingrays to eat. Divers have seen hammerheads with poisonous stingray barbs sticking out of their mouths, tongues, and throats. Those stinging barbs just don't seem to bother a hammerhead. One diver saw a hammerhead with ninety-six barbs in its mouth!

Just a few pools of water—but enough for some fish!

Chapter Four

Strange Ways of Breathing

You probably know that a fish uses its gills to breathe underwater. The gills of most fish are on each side of the head. They are filled with tiny blood vessels that absorb oxygen out of the water, and get rid of carbon dioxide from the bloodstream of the fish. Young amphibians, such as tadpoles, also have gills. Some fish have more than just gills, though. Did you know that some fishes have lungs too?

A Look at the Lungfish

The lungfish has gills like other fishes, but it has another way to breathe, too. Most fishes have a **swim bladder** inside their bodies that is filled with air and helps them stay afloat. The lungfish has one or two swim bladders that are lined with blood vessels. These blood vessels act like a lung, absorbing oxygen from the air that the lungfish swallows.

If there is plenty of oxygen in the water, a lungfish breathes mostly through its gills. In the muddy waters where African lungfish live, though, there isn't always enough oxygen in the water to keep the fish alive. So the lungfish just rises to the surface and gulps air.

Most fishes have two-chambered hearts to pump blood to and from the gills and around the rest of its body. Because the lungfish has a lung, it needs a more complicated heart with

A lungfish goes to the surface for air.

four chambers. A partition in its heart separates the two extra chambers that circulate blood to and from the lungs as well as the gills.

During the wet months, African lungfish hunt fish and frogs in rivers. In the hot African summer, the rivers dry up, but the lungfish can still survive. Just before the dry season begins, a lungfish burrows into the mud. It uses its mouth and body to widen the bottom of its burrow until it can turn around. Then its skin produces a thick slime that mixes with the mud and forms a cocoon around the lungfish. The lungfish lies dormant in this cocoon until the rains fall again.

Before it becomes dormant, the lungfish makes a tiny hole in the cocoon near its mouth, with a small tube leading up to the surface. Through that tiny hole the patient lungfish gets just enough oxygen to breathe, but not so much that it dries out. It can survive for months in its burrow until the rainy season comes. Then rain dissolves the cocoon, and the lungfish comes out. It looks dry and shriveled at first, but it slowly absorbs water until it looks normal again. If it has to, a lungfish can survive in its cocoon for up to 4 years.

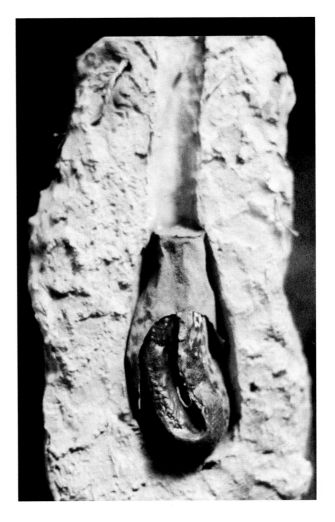

An African lungfish rests in its mud cocoon.

Arapaimas

The arapaima of South America has lungs too. Its swim bladder, which is joined to its throat, is lined with blood vessels that absorb oxygen directly from the air. This is a great advantage for the arapaima because the waters of the Amazon River where it lives often don't contain enough oxygen for a fish to breathe with gills. That doesn't bother the arapaima, though. It just swims to the surface and gulps air when it needs to.

This large arapaima can breathe air.

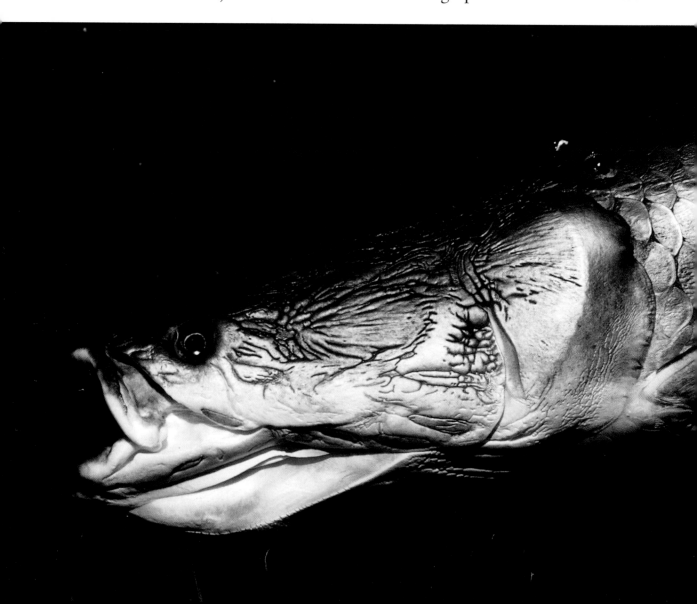

Because arapaimas have lungs, they can survive in still-water, and **stagnant** swamps too. At breeding time they hide in these swamps and spawn. Then they dig shallow nests to lay their eggs and guard their young. The swamp is a safe place because the slow-moving water doesn't contain enough oxygen for many of the arapaima's predators.

Arapaimas are members of a family of fish called "bony tongues." Although they have teeth in their jaws, these fish

generally bite their prey with their tongue! They have bones in their tongue with teeth sticking out, and have teeth on the roof of their mouth, too. To bite their prey, they press their bony, toothed tongue against the teeth in the roof of their mouths and crunch.

The arapaima has another claim to fame—it is the biggest freshwater fish in the world—up to 10 feet (3 m) long. Sadly, people have killed so many of the largest ones, that very large arapaimas are now rare.

Ropefish

The snakelike ropefish of Africa also has a set of primitive lungs. It can live up to 8 hours out of the water!

A walking catfish crosses a dirt road in Florida.

Chapter Five

Like a Fish Out of Water

Amphibians such as frogs and salamanders spend part of the time in the water and part on land. Penguins nest on land, but spend most of their time hunting underwater. While you might once have thought that fishes were supposed to spend their entire lives in the water, it probably won't surprise you by now to learn that there are fishes that don't follow this rule either. Despite all the problems a fish out of water has to overcome, some fishes venture out on land.

The Marvelous Mudskipper

The mudskipper not only walks on land, it spends more time on land than in the water. This fish has pectoral fins that are large and muscular enough to use as stubby legs. It can move these strong fins forward, backward, and sideways. To get around the mudflats at low tide, a mudskipper does something called "crutching." It thrusts its pectoral fins forward while resting its weight on its pelvic fins, and then pulls itself forward with its pectorals.

That may sound like a slow and laborious way to get around, but a mudskipper can actually move along at quite a clip. In fact, it can hop along faster than a human can walk! Sometimes it flips itself forward by curling its body sideways and suddenly straightening it out. A mudskipper can leap up to 24 inches (60 cm) this way.

Mudskippers bask in the sun.

How does a mudskipper breathe on land? It has no lungs, but it has lots of other tricks. It stores water in spongy sacs around its gills and in its mouth, so it has an oxygen-filled water supply that lasts a long time. Every now and then it replaces the stale water with fresh water full of oxygen from a puddle. In addition, it can absorb oxygen through bumps on its skin and tail. When it basks in the sun, this fish hangs its tail in the water to soak up extra oxygen. It breathes with the wet lining of its mouth and tongue too. That is why you may see a mudskipper resting with its mouth wide open.

Mudskippers need to protect their delicate eyes from the sand and sun, so their eyes are covered with a thick layer of clear skin. A fish has no tear ducts, so the mudskipper rolls its eyes back in its eye sockets occasionally to keep them moist.

A mudskipper can see both in the air and underwater.

Over time, mudskippers have developed a technique for solving another problem of land travel—how to see in the air. A fish's eyes are made for underwater vision, but they don't work so well out of the water. Most fish would be nearsighted in the air, but mudskippers can change the shape of their lenses and corneas so that they can see either in water or on land. They have such good land vision that they can catch an insect as it flies through the air.

When the tide comes in, mudskippers retreat into burrows they have dug in the mud. These burrows are quite elaborate, with an enlarged chamber at the end. Mudskippers fight for burrow space, and there are always some—usually young fish—that don't get a burrow. To escape from big hungry fish brought in by the tide, mudskippers without burrows climb up into the mangrove trees.

When the tide goes out again, mudskippers wander over the mudflats, searching for insects, worms, and other prey. They often climb up stems and roots and over mud banks to find a meal. They have no trouble being "fish out of water!"

Cling Fishes

The Chilean cling fish of South America isn't as athletic as the mudskipper, but it also spends a lot of time out of water. It has a different way of breathing. A special patch of skin on its belly is full of blood vessels. When the cling fish needs to breathe, it raises the front part of its body off the rocks and takes in oxygen through this patch. It has a backup system. The cling fish can also hold air in its mouth and absorb oxygen through the moist lining.

To keep cool in the hot sunshine, the Chilean cling fish stays perfectly still. That way it doesn't create extra heat. Every so often, a wave washes over the fish and cools it down. Then it can move about again, searching for food along the shore.

In cloudy weather, this fish can stay on land for about 2 days without losing too much moisture. If the sun drives its temperature above 75 degrees Fahrenheit (24 degrees Celsius), though, the cling fish will die.

The cling fishes get their name from another unusual adaptation. Their pelvic fins are fused together to make a suction pad. They use this suction pad to cling to rocks near the shore so the waves don't knock them about.

Climbing Perch

The climbing perch was discovered and named by a Dutch naturalist in the eighteenth century. He found one of these fish 5 feet (1.5 m) up in a palm tree in South America. The fish

A climbing perch can survive in stagnant water.

was bathing in a trickle of water running down the trunk, but it probably didn't get there on its own. Though other people have found the climbing perch in trees, too, it is unlikely that they actually climb. Scientists think it is more likely that these fish were dropped there accidentally by a bird that planned to have them for dinner.

A climbing perch can last a long time out of water because it has a special breathing system. It has hollow structures lined with blood vessels at the top of its gill chambers. These structures are very complicated, like a labyrinth, which is why the

44

members of this fish family are known as "labyrinth fish." As a climbing perch grows, these breathing organs become even more complex. The added twists and folds give the organs more surface area, and the perch can get even more oxygen.

A climbing perch's gills are not very efficient, so it needs to rise to the water's surface often in order to breathe. If it can't get to the surface, it suffocates. Thanks to its special breathing apparatus, though, it can survive in water that doesn't contain much oxygen.

If the water gets too stagnant, a climbing perch crawls onto land and sets off in search of cleaner water. It travels over land by raising itself up in front on its pectoral fins and gill covers and pushing forward with its tail. It just flops along over stones and sticks until it finally finds a new pond.

Kissing Gouramis

These air-breathing cousins of the climbing perch aren't really kissing. They're two males trying to scare each other away.

Amazing Archerfish

Archerfish live in the streams of India, Malaysia, and Australia. They can't breathe out of the water, or walk about on land, yet they hunt prey that is out of the water. An archerfish shoots a stream of water at an insect and knocks it into the water, so that the archerfish can eat it. An archerfish could really be called a "spitting fish."

This archerfish has excellent aim.

The archerfish has a special groove in the roof of its mouth. To shoot down an insect, it first snaps its gill covers shut, to compress water in its mouth and gill chambers. Then it presses its tongue against the groove, forming a tube. Then it shoots!

It's hard to see an insect in the air accurately from underwater. The surface of the water bends the light, so that, from underwater, the insect looks as though it is in a different place. The archerfish solves this problem by learning to aim above the spot where the insect appears to be. Baby archerfish begin practicing almost as soon as they are born—it takes a lot of practice to become a sharpshooter. An adult archerfish can hit an insect perched 5 feet (1.5 m) above it.

Other Fishes Out of Water

A few other fishes can survive out of water, at least for a while. The bullhead, which is a kind of catfish, can "swim" through grass—if the grass is wet. Electric eels sometimes have to cross land to get from one pool to another. They slither like snakes on land. Out of water, they can actually use their gills to breathe air.

Walking catfish, which came originally from Southeast Asia, flourish in Florida. They sometimes surprise local residents by wriggling across the road in droves, searching for fresh water. Tree-shaped breathing organs in the top of their gill chambers help them survive on land. They move along the ground as an eel does, and use the spines of their pectoral fins to brace themselves as they slither along.

*This striped burrfish
certainly is oddly
shaped.*

Chapter Six

A Fishy Finale

The fish world has so many exceptions to the rules that you begin to wonder what the rules are. You've learned about fishes that move around on land, fishes that give birth to their young in unusual ways, and fishes that have unusual shapes.

Now that you are familiar with some of the funny fishes in the world, maybe you have different ideas of what a fish is. Next time someone asks you, "What is a fish?" maybe you'll have new answers. You might say, "*Most* fishes have scales

49

and fins," or "*Many* fishes have long, streamlined bodies." It would be correct to say, "*Most* fishes lay their eggs in the water," and "*Most* fishes live all their lives in the water and breathe with gills."

Then you might go on to describe some of the weird and wonderful fish that break the rules. If you ever thought fish were boring and all pretty much the same—now you know!

Funny Fishes Around the World

Common name	Scientific name	Where found
Filipino dwarf pygmy goby	*Pandaka pygmaea*	Fresh water in the Philippines
Whale shark	*Rhincodon typus*	Around the world near the equator
Sea horse	*Hippocampus* spp. (35 species)	Shallow coastal temperate and tropical waters
Pipefish	*Syngnathus* spp. (150 species)	Marine, brackish, and freshwater coastal habitats
Leafy seadragon	*Phllopteryx eques*	Off Australian coast
Boxfish	*Lactophrys* sp.	Tropical ocean waters
Pufferfish	over 100 species	Tropical waters in Atlantic, Pacific and Indian oceans
Garden eel	*Gorgasia sillneri*	Tropical waters
Electric eel	*Electrophorus electricus*	Amazon River basin and the Orinoco River
Toad fish	family *Batrachoididae* (64 species)	Western Atlantic from Maine to the West Indies
Gulper eel	*Eurypharynx pelecanoides*	Deep ocean, 500 to 3000 m down
Stonefish	*Synanceja* sp.	Tropical marine waters from South Africa east to Japan, Australia
Hagfish	*Myxine* sp.	All temperate seas and the North Atlantic
Banded yellow mouthbrooder	*Tilapia mossambica*	Rivers and lakes of eastern Africa

continued next page

Funny Fishes Around the World *continued*

Common name	Scientific name	Where found
Arawana	*Osteoglossum bicirrhosum*	Brazil, Colombia, Peru
Hammerhead shark	*Sphyrna* spp. (10 species)	Tropical waters worldwide
Spiny dogfish	*Squalus acanthius*	Temperate and subarctic North Atlantic and North Pacific oceans
African lungfish	genus *Protopterus*	Africa
Arapaima or pirarucú	*Arapaima gigas*	Amazon River basin
Ropefish or reedfish	*Erpetoichthys calabaricus*	Fresh and brackish waters of Western Africa
Mudskipper	*Periophthalmus* spp.	Coastal mangrove swamps of Africa, Indian and Pacific Oceans
Chilean cling fish	family *Gobiesocidae*	South America
Walking catfish	*Clarias batrachus*	Originally Southeast Asia, India. Now in Florida
Climbing perch	*Anabas testudineus*	Originally Southeast Asia, India. Now in Gulf of Mexico, South America
Archerfish	*Toxotes jaculatrix*	Southeast Asia to the western Pacific
Kissing gourami	Family *Helostomatidae*	Thailand and Java
Bullheads	*Ictalurus* spp.	Freshwaters in most of the USA

Glossary

algae—small plants without roots or stems that grow in water or damp places

anal fin—a fin on the rear of a fish's underside near its tail

carapace—a bony case covering the back of certain animals, including the box fish

dorsal fin—a single fin in the center of a fish's back

embryo—an unborn or unhatched animal in an early stage of development

evolve—to change slowly over generations, developing specialized physical characteristics or behaviors

fertilize—to combine sperm and egg to make a new organism

fishes—the plural form of "fish" used to describe two or more species

gills—body parts that filter oxygen out of water

milt—the sperm-containing fluid produced by a male fish

parasite—an organism that feeds on another living organism

pectoral fins—paired fins on the forward sides of a fish

pelvic fins—paired fins on the rear sides of a fish

placenta—a structure full of blood vessels that nourishes the unborn young in the uterus

predator—an animal that hunts another animal

prey—an animal hunted by another animal for food

scales—thin, transparent plates that cover a fish's body

sinus—a cavity inside an animal's body

stagnant—still water or very slow-moving water

swim bladder—an air-filled sac inside a fish's body that helps it stay afloat

vertebrate—an animal that has a backbone

To Find Out More

Books

Bailey, Jill. *Fish*. New York: Facts on File, 1990.

Broekel, Ray. *Dangerous Fish*. Danbury, CT: Children's Press, 1982.

Lovett, Sara. *Extremely Weird Fish*. Santa Fe, NM: John Muir Publications, 1996.

Parker, Steve. *Fish*. New York: Knopf, 1990.

Seward, Homer. *Eels*. New York: Rourke Book Co., 1998.

Snedden, Robert. *What Is a Fish?* San Francisco: Sierra Club Juveniles, 1993.

Swinney, Geoff. *Fish Facts*. Gretna, LA: Pelican Publishing Co., 1994.

Welsbacher, Anne. *Hammerhead Sharks*. Mankato, MN: Capstone Press, 1998.

Organizations and Online Sites

Cichlid Research Home Page
http://cichlidresearch.com
This site provides lots of information on these popular fishes.

Cyber School-Marine Life
http://www.iinet.au/~edubooks/CyberMarin.html
This site provides information on many fishes and other marine life, including sea horses and file fishes.

GeoZoo: Earth Safari
http://www.geobop.com/geozoo
This site offers GeoReports, GeoCharts, and quick facts about a wide variety of animals.

North American Native Fishes Association
http://www.nanfa.org
This organization is dedicated to the enjoyment, study, and conservation of the North American continent's native fishes.

U.S. Fish and Wildlife Service

http://www.fws.gov

This United States government agency has information on endangered species, habitat conservation, and more.

A Note on Sources

The first thing I did when I began this book was to sift through my memories. Over the years I have taken numerous courses in natural history and visited dozens of aquariums around the country. Thinking about those experiences gave me more ideas of weird and wonderful fish to include. My next step was to browse through my personal nature library for more ideas and facts. Palmer and Fowler's *Handbook of Natural History*, even though it is old-fashioned and incomplete, gave me leads about various species to include.

Then it's off to the library for more books. The two I finally relied on most heavily were *Fish* by Steve Parker and *The Encyclopedia of Aquatic Life* edited by Keith Bannister and Andrew Campbell. The first is a children's book but it has easy-to-access information, and great pictures! The second is a rather heavy volume and not especially readable, but it is full of detailed and accurate information.

Once I knew which species I wanted to include, I went to the Internet. Most of the information on fish is for aquarium enthusiasts, but, if I searched patiently for a specific genus and species, I often got useful information. A good site turned out to be the *Cyber School–Marine Life* site.

The help of expert consultant Ron Coleman, Ph.D., at the University of California in Davis, California, was invaluable in creating this book.

—*Sara Swan Miller*

Index

Numbers in *italics* indicate illustrations.

About the Author

Sara Swan Miller has enjoyed working with children all her life, first as a Montessori nursery school teacher, and later as an outdoor environmental educator at the Mohonk Preserve in New Paltz, New York. As director of the school program at the preserve, she has taught hundreds of schoolchildren the importance of appreciating and respecting the natural world.

She has written over thirty books, including *Three Stories You Can Read to Your Dog*; *Three Stories You Can Read to Your Cat*; *Three More Stories You Can Read to Your Dog*; and *What's in the Woods?: An Outdoor Activity Book*, as well as four other books on strange animals for the Watts Library.

She has also written several books on farm animals for Children's Press's *True Books* series, and many books on animals for Franklin Watts's *Animals in Order* series, including ones on true bugs, flies, rodents, perching birds, turtles, and salamanders.